APERTURE MASTERS OF PHOTOGRAPHY

APERTURE MASTERS OF PHOTOGRAPHY

MANUEL ALVAREZ BRAVO

KÖNEMANN

Acknowledgments/Danksagung/Remerciements:
Manuel Alvarez Bravo, the International Center of Photography, New York, and the Witkin Gallery, New York, for the use of original prints from which to reproduce, and to Manuel Alvarez Bravo, Colette Alvarez Urbajtel, Eugenia Rendon de Olazabal, and Cornell Capa

This 1997 edition is a coproduction of
Könemann Verlags GmbH, Bonner Str. 126, D-50968 Cologne
and Aperture Foundation, Inc.

Subscribe to *Aperture*, the Quarterly, for just $50 U.S. for one year or $86 U.S. for two years and you'll also receive a FREE copy of *Edward Weston: The Flame of Recognition* with your paid subscription. Write or email now to reserve your free book, a $27.50 value. APERTURE 20 East 23rd Street, Dept. 447 New York, NY 10010. Email: Circulation@Aperture.org. Or fax credit card orders to (212) 475-8790.

German translation: Ulrike Bischoff
French translation: Jacques Bosser
Typesetting: Oliver Hessmann
Coordination: Sylvia Hecken
Cover design: Peter Feierabend
Production manager: Detlev Schaper
Printing and binding: Sing Cheong Printing Co. Ltd.
Printed in Hong Kong, China

ISBN 3-89508-606-1
10 9 8 7 6 5 4 3 2

"[Manuel Alvarez Bravo's] work is rooted firmly in his love and compassionate understanding of his own country, its people, their problems and their needs. These he has never ceased to explore and to know intimately... He wishes to speak with warmth about Mexico as Atget spoke about Paris."

Paul Strand

»[Manuel Alvarez Bravos] Werk ist tief verwurzelt in seiner Liebe und seinem einfühlsamen Verständnis für sein Land, sein Volk, dessen Schwierigkeiten und Bedürfnisse. Sie zu erforschen und eingehend kennenzulernen hat er niemals aufgehört... Sein Anliegen ist es, mit einer Wärme von Mexiko zu erzählen, wie Atget von Paris erzählt hat.«

Paul Strand

« L'œuvre [de Manuel Alvarez Bravo] est fermement enracinée dans son amour plein de compassion et de compréhension pour son pays, son peuple, leurs problèmes et leurs besoins. Il n'a jamais cessé d'explorer cette matière et la connaît de la façon la plus intime... Il souhaite nous parler avec chaleur du Mexique, comme Atget l'a fait de Paris. »

Paul Strand

"[Manuel Alvarez Bravo's] photographs were enigmas in black and white, silent yet eloquent: without saying it, they alluded to other realities, and without showing them, they evoked other images."

Octavio Paz

»[Manuel Alvarez Bravos] Fotografien waren Rätsel in Schwarz und Weiß. Still und doch beredt: Ohne es zu sagen, spielten sie auf andere Realitäten an, und ohne sie zu zeigen, riefen sie andere Bilder wach.«

Octavio Paz

« Les photographies [de Manuel Alvarez Bravo] étaient des énigmes en noir et blanc, silencieuses mais néanmoins éloquentes : sans le dire, elles faisaient allusion à d'autres réalités, et sans les montrer évoquaient d'autres images. »

Octavio Paz

THE INDIGENOUS VISION OF MANUEL ALVAREZ BRAVO

Popular Art is the art of the People.

A popular painter is an artisan who, as in the Middle Ages, remains anonymous. His work needs no advertisement, as it is done for the people around him. The more pretentious artist craves to become famous, and it is characteristic of his work that it is bought for the name rather than for the work – a name that is built up by propaganda.

Before the Conquest all art was of the people, and popular art has never ceased to exist in Mexico. The art called Popular is quite fugitive in character, of sensitive and personal quality, with less of the impersonal and intellectual characteristics that are the essence of the art of the schools. It is the work of talent nourished by personal experience and by that of the community—rather than being taken from the experiences of other painters in other times and other cultures, which forms the intellectual chain of nonpopular art.

Manuel Alvarez Bravo

The resonance of credo is unmistakable. Coming from a photographer, these words[1] do not proclaim a personal achievement, but they do indicate his aspirations for

MANUEL ALVAREZ BRAVOS VISION EINER VOLKSKUNST

Volkskunst ist die Kunst des Volkes.

Ein Volksmaler ist ein Künstler, der wie im Mittelalter anonym bleibt. Sein Werk braucht keine Werbung, da es für die Menschen um ihn herum geschaffen ist. Der ehrgeizigere Künstler strebt danach, berühmt zu werden, und seine Arbeit wird eher um des Namens als um des Werkes willen gekauft – eines Namens, der durch Propaganda aufgebaut wird.

Vor der Eroberung war alle Kunst die des Volkes, und in Mexiko hat die Volkskunst nie zu existieren aufgehört. Die sogenannte Volkskunst ist ihrem Wesen nach recht flüchtig, empfindlich und persönlich und hat weniger jene unpersönlichen und intellektuellen Merkmale, die den Kern der akademischen Kunst ausmachen. Sie ist das Werk von Talenten, die sich aus dem persönlichen Erleben und dem der Gemeinschaft speisen – statt aus der Erfahrung anderer Maler anderer Zeiten oder anderer Kulturen, die die intellektuelle Kette der akademischen Kunst bilden.

Manuel Alvarez Bravo

Unmißverständlich klingt hier das Glaubensbekenntnis durch. Von einem Fotografen stammend[1], proklamieren diese Worte keine persönliche Leistung, sondern verweisen auf

LA VISION INDIGÈNE DE MANUEL ALVAREZ BRAVO

L'art populaire est l'art du peuple.

Un peintre populaire est un artisan qui, comme au Moyen-Âge, reste anonyme. Son travail n'a pas besoin de publicité, puisqu'il est fait pour les gens qui l'entourent. L'artiste plus prétentieux s'efforce de devenir célèbre, et son œuvre est plus achetée pour son nom que pour son travail – nom construit par la propagande.

Avant la Conquête, tout art était populaire, et cette forme artistique n'a jamais cessé d'exister au Mexique. L'art appelé « populaire » est de caractère assez fugitif, pénétré de qualités sensibles et personnelles, mais moins imbu de ces caractéristiques impersonnelles et intellectuelles qui sont l'essence de l'art des écoles. Il est l'œuvre d'un talent nourri par l'expérience personnelle et par celle d'une communauté, au lieu que d'être tiré de l'expérience d'autres peintres, d'autres époques et d'autres cultures, qui forment les chaînes intellectuelles dans lesquelles s'enferme l'art non populaire.

Manuel Alvarez Bravo

La résonance de ce credo est évidente. Venant d'un photographe, ces mots[1] ne proclament pas une réussite personnelle, mais désignent les aspirations qu'il assigne à son art.

photography. Yet Manuel Alvarez Bravo, at long last becoming more widely known outside his native country and the professional world of photography, has in the past sixty years forged a body of work precisely to meet such standards: fugitive, sensitive, personal, nourished by experience, deeply rooted in his culture and his people.

For an image-maker whose work has been known to and admired by Henri Cartier-Bresson, Edward Weston, Paul Strand, Diego Rivera, and André Breton, remaining comparatively obscure through the course of almost two-thirds of a century's work in his chosen medium is no mean feat. One cannot help but suspect that to some extent this is self-imposed, born of a 'fugitive' or reticent nature and a consistent avoidance of personal publicity. Insofar as it appears to be voluntary, I find myself loath to violate that privacy.

Yet there are other factors to consider. One of these is his remarkable absence, until very recently, from virtually all the standard reference works on photographic history. (Indeed, he remains unmentioned in even the very latest edition of Beaumont Newhall's 'magnum opus'.) Some attention

seine Erwartungen an die Fotografie. Manuel Alvarez Bravo, der endlich auch außerhalb seines Heimatlandes und der professionellen Welt der Fotografie größere Bekanntheit erlangt, hat in den letzten sechzig Jahren ein Werk geschaffen, das diesen Erwartungen entspricht: flüchtig, sensibel, persönlich, geprägt von Erfahrungen, tief in seiner Kultur und seinem Volk verwurzelt.

Für einen Bilder-Macher, dessen Werk Henri Cartier-Bresson, Edward Weston, Paul Strand, Diego Rivera und André Breton kannten und bewunderten, ist es bemerkenswert, im Laufe eines Schaffens, das sich über fast zwei Drittel eines Jahrhunderts erstreckt, vergleichsweise unbekannt zu bleiben. Man kann nicht umhin zu vermuten, daß dies bis zu einem gewissen Grad selbst gewählt ist und einer Abneigung gegen Publizität entspringt. Insoweit diese Privatheit anscheinend dem eigenen Willen entspringt, widerstrebt es mir, sie zu verletzen.

Und doch sind noch andere Faktoren zu berücksichtigen. Einer davon ist die bemerkenswerte Tatsache, daß er bis vor kurzem in praktisch keinem Standardwerk zur Geschichte der Fotografie erwähnt wurde. (Selbst in der neuesten Auflage des ›magnum opus‹ von Beaumont Newhall bleibt

Manuel Alvarez Bravo, qui commence enfin à être largement connu hors de son pays natal et du monde de la photographie professionnelle, a forgé au cours des soixante dernières années une œuvre qui répond précisément à de tels standards : fugitivité, sensibilité, personnalité, appui sur l'expérience, profondément enracinée dans sa culture et son peuple.

Pour un créateur d'images dont les œuvres ont été connues d'Henri Cartier-Bresson, Edward Weston, Paul Strand, Diego Rivera et André Breton et admirées par eux, rester relativement obscur tout au long d'une carrière qui couvre presque les deux tiers du siècle dans le médium qu'il avait choisi n'est pas sans importance. On ne peut s'empêcher de suspecter que dans une certaine mesure, ceci a été voulu, est le fruit d'une nature fuyante ou réticente et du rejet constant de toute publicité personnelle. Cette attitude étant volontaire, je me trouve moi-même gêné de violer cette intimité.

D'autres facteurs sont cependant à prendre en considération. L'un d'entre eux est l'étonnante absence du photographe, jusqu'à une date très récente, de pratiquement toutes les grandes œuvres de référence sur l'histoire de la photographie. (Il n'est

Parábola optica, 1931

seems in order, if only to acknowledge what has been achieved. Additionally, his work assumes that photography is an explicitly demotic visual language, to whose fullest progressive range he is committed.

This is not to be understood as 'socialist realism' in any sense. Alvarez Bravo's imagery does not deal in stereotypes; his awareness of and response to the ethos of Mexican culture is far too complex and multi-leveled to permit such over-simplification. There is a commitment to people on the lower social strata inherent in the persistent address of Alvarez Bravo's vision to their experience, and implicit in his uninterest in the middle and upper classes. Certainly this is intentional, and emblematic of his politics. But the work is free of slogans and generalities. Viewers of photographs may tend to generalize from them – sometimes at the photographer's instigation, often independently, and always at their own risk. But one of photography's unique functions is to describe particulars. That aspect of the medium is essential to Alvarez Bravo, for he uses photography as a probe, an incisive tool for uncovering the heart of a culture embodied in the individual people who form its base.

er ungenannt.) Eine gewisse Beachtung scheint hier angebracht, und sei es nur, um das Erreichte anzuerkennen. Zudem entspringt sein Werk der Idee, daß die Fotografie eine explizit volkstümliche visuelle Sprache ist. Ihrer Verbreitung ist er verpflichtet.

Das ist in keiner Weise als ›sozialistischer Realismus‹ zu verstehen. Alvarez Bravos Bilder befassen sich nicht mit Stereotypen; sein Bewußtsein für die Wesensart der mexikanischen Kultur ist viel zu komplex und vielschichtig, um eine solche Vereinfachung zuzulassen. Aus der Tatsache, daß Alvarez Bravo seinen Blick ausschließlich auf die Erfahrung von Menschen der unteren sozialen Schichten richtet, spricht implizit eine Verpflichtung gegenüber diesen Menschen. Das ist sicher beabsichtigt und kennzeichnend für seine Weltanschauung. Allerdings ist sein Werk frei von Parolen und Allgemeinplätzen. Betrachter seiner Fotografien mögen zu Verallgemeinerungen neigen – manchmal angestiftet vom Fotografen, oft von sich aus und immer auf eigene Gefahr. Doch eine der einzigartigen Funktionen der Fotografie besteht in der Darstellung von Besonderheiten. Dieser Aspekt des Mediums ist für Alvarez Bravo entscheidend, denn er benutzt die Fotografie als Sonde, um das Herz

toujours pas mentionné dans la toute dernière édition du ‹ magnum opus › de Beaumont Newhall.) Il semble donc qu'il faille enfin regarder cette œuvre, ne serait-ce que pour reconnaître ce qui a été accompli ici. Par ailleurs, ce travail suppose que la photographie est un langage visuel explicitement populaire, et son auteur s'est engagé dans l'aile la plus progressiste de ce mouvement.

Il ne s'agit en aucune façon de ‹ réalisme socialiste ›. Les images d'Alvarez Bravo ne font pas appel à des stéréotypes ; sa manière d'appréhender et de réagir donne des formes beaucoup trop complexes à l'éthique de la culture mexicaine et n'autorise une telle simplification autorises. On trouve un engagement envers le peuple des couches sociales inférieures, dans l'attention permanente que la vision d'Alvarez Bravo porte à leur existence, et a contrario dans son manque d'intérêt pour les classes bourgeoises et supérieures. Ceci est certainement intentionnel et représentatif de sa pensée politique. Mais l'œuvre est libre de slogans et de généralités. Ceux qui regardent ces photographies peuvent tenter de généraliser à partir d'elles, parfois à l'instigation de leur auteur, souvent indépendamment de lui, mais toujours à leurs propres risques.

La hija de los danzantes, 1933

In referring to photography as a demotic language, then, I am not suggesting the establishment of some simplified, standardized politico-visual code and its imposition on all those who would communicate through photographs. Put it this way: there are many dialects at the disposal of the photographer; his/her choice thereof is also a choice of audience. To speak in the language of the elite, the hieratic form of a language (Mandarin in China, for instance) is to restrict one's messages to a particular class. Voicing one's thoughts in the common tongue, the demotic, points them in the opposite direction. With Alvarez Bravo, we have someone who – to extend the linguistic analogy – is fluent in both Mandarin and Cantonese, but chooses the latter to convey his messages.

einer Kultur freizulegen, das in den einzelnen Menschen, die ihre Basis bilden, verkörpert ist.

Indem ich die Fotografie als populäre Sprache bezeichne, möchte ich also keinesfalls für die Einführung eines simplifizierten, standardisierten, politisch-visuellen Codes eintreten, den jeder, der durch Fotografien kommuniziert, zu benutzen hätte. Ich will damit sagen, daß es viele Dialekte gibt, die dem Fotografen zur Verfügung stehen; für welchen er oder sie sich entscheidet, beinhaltet zugleich eine Auswahl des Publikums. Die Sprache der Elite zu sprechen, also die feierliche Form einer Sprache (im Chinesischen zum Beispiel Mandarin), heißt, die eigene Botschaft auf eine bestimmte Schicht zu beschränken. Seine Gedanken in der Umgangssprache, der populären Sprache, zu formulieren, deutet in die entgegengesetzte Richtung. In Alvarez Bravo haben wir einen Menschen, der – um die linguistische Analogie auszuweiten – sowohl Mandarin als auch Kantonesisch fließend beherrscht, sich aber für das letztere entscheidet, um seine Botschaften zu vermitteln.

L'une des fonctions spécifiques de la photographie est de représenter des individus. Cet aspect du médium est essentiel pour Alvarez Bravo qui utilise la photographie comme une sonde, outil incisif qui lui permet de découvrir le cœur d'une culture incarnée dans les individus qui forment sa base.

Lorsque je parle de la photographie comme d'un langage populaire, je ne suggère pas d'établir quelque code politico-visuel simplifié et standardisé ni de l'imposer à tous ceux qui voudraient communiquer par les photographies. Disons que de nombreux dialectes sont à la disposition du photographe. Son choix dans ce domaine est également un choix d'audience. Pour parler dans le langage de l'élite, la forme hiératique d'un langage (le mandarin en Chine, par exemple) est de restreindre la compréhension des messages à une classe sociale particulière. Exprimer ses pensées dans la langue commune – démotique – leur ouvre un tout autre horizon. Avec Alvarez Bravo, nous avons quelqu'un qui – pour poursuivre l'analogie linguistique – parle couramment le mandarin et le cantonnais, mais choisit ce dernier pour véhiculer ses messages.

Paisaje y galope, 1932

That is an illuminating and instructive stance for a photographer to adopt. It merits scrutiny at this juncture because the definition of photography is currently being reshaped by a variety of cultural forces. One of those forces is the contemporary art world, whose relationship to photography at present might best be described as carpetbagging. In the art world microcosm, two theories contend for supremacy. The first, an aloof formalism, argues for the self-referentiality of creative activity; its postulate is that "in the last analysis the main subject matter of art is art." Ostensibly antagonistic to this position, yet not all that far from it, is the fashionable despair of postmodernism, whose thesis is that artistic invention (if it ever existed) is now exhausted, leaving no alternative but endless recycling; it is a cynical vision of culture as flea market, artist as shopper. Something may be learned by assessing these notions in light of an approach to photography that is integral to its medium yet at the same time directly contradicts both of them.

Dies ist für einen Fotografen eine erhellende und lehrreiche Haltung. Sie verdient eine genauere Überprüfung, da sich die Fotografie gegenwärtig wegen der Vielzahl kultureller Einflüsse neu definiert. Besonders hervorzuheben ist hier die bildende Kunst und ihr Verhältnis zur Fotografie. Zwei Theorien ringen im Moment um die Vorherrschaft in der Kunstwelt. Die Vertreter eines distanzierten Formalismus postulieren die Selbstbezogenheit des schöpferischen Aktes: »Der Hauptgegenstand der Kunst ist letzten Endes die Kunst.« Scheinbar antagonistisch, in Wahrheit aber nicht allzu weit davon entfernt, ist die modische Verzweiflung der Postmoderne, die die These vertritt, daß die künstlerische Erfindungsgabe (wenn es sie denn je gab) heute erschöpft ist, was keine andere Alternative als ein endloses Recycling zuläßt – eine zynische Sicht von der Kultur als einem Flohmarkt, auf dem der Künstler als Käufer auftritt. Es mag durchaus dienlich sein, diese Vorstellungen an einem Herangehen an die Fotografie zu messen, das unerläßlicher Bestandteil dieses Mediums ist, zugleich aber beiden Sichtweisen widerspricht.

Pour un photographe, cette attitude est éclairante et instructive. Elle mérite d'être analysée sur ce point précis car la définition de la photographie est actuellement soumise à une sérieuse remise en cause par de multiples forces culturelles. L'une de ces forces est le monde de l'art contemporain, dont la relation avec la photographie relève du discours de préaux électoraux. Dans ce microcosme, deux théories prétendent à la suprématie. La première, un formalisme distant, veut que l'activité artistique soit autoréférentielle. Elle postule que « le principal sujet de l'art en dernière analyse est l'art. » Le désespoir élégant du postmodernisme reste ostensiblement antagoniste et défend la thèse que l'invention artistique (si elle a jamais existé) est dorénavant épuisée, ne laissant d'autre alternative qu'un « recyclage » sans fin. Il s'agit là d'une vision cynique qui fait de la culture un marché aux puces, et de l'artiste un chaland. On peut cependant tirer quelques éléments intéressants de l'évaluation de ces notions à la lumière d'une approche de la photographie qui appartient pleinement à ce médium, tout en les contredisant toutes les deux.

Los agachados, 1932–34

The purposefulness of that contradiction is made quite explicit in the statement from Alvarez Bravo quoted at the beginning of this essay. We are face to face here not with a naïf artist, but with an intentionally indigenous vision.

The distinction is significant. Cumulatively, Alvarez Bravo's deceptively simple images form themselves into a mosaic, an expansive lyric suite or tone poem. This poet's style is one of quiet, conversational intimacy, eschewing bravura, its virtuosity subsumed under the rhythms of a gradual unfolding. Here is one of those bodies of work that requires the viewer to step into what a colleague of mine calls a 'bubble of slow time' – in this case, a particularly heat-baked, sun-soaked, thick-shadowed, southern-hemisphere variety of slow time.

Like his craftsmanship, his sophistication conceals itself. Yet it is apparent – from images such as *Un poco alegre y graciosa* [Somewhat gay and graceful, page 71] and *La buena fama durmiendo* [Good reputation sleeping, front cover] – that he is adept in both the responsive mode, as in Cartier-Bresson, and the directorial mode of photography, as in Meatyard. Other images (*Los agachados* [The crouched ones, page 15], *Retrato desagradable*

Daß dieser Widerspruch beabsichtigt ist, wird in Alvarez Bravos oben zitierter Äußerung sehr deutlich. Wir haben es hier nicht mit einem naiven Künstler zu tun, sondern mit einer bewußt volkstümlichen Sicht.

Der Unterschied liegt klar auf der Hand. Alvarez Bravos scheinbar einfachen Bilder setzen sich zu einem komplexen Mosaik zusammen, einer umfassenden lyrischen Suite oder Tondichtung. Der Stil dieses Dichters besteht in einer beredten, aber dennoch zurückhaltenden Intimität, die ihre Virtuosität erst allmählich entfaltet. Wir haben es hier mit einem jener Werke zu tun, das vom Betrachter verlangt, sich in ›eine Zeitlupen-Luftblase‹ zu begeben, wie einer meiner Kollegen es nennt – und zwar in diesem Fall eine ausgedörrte, sonnendurchtränkte, tiefumschattete, südliche Variante der Zeitlupe.

Seine technische Raffinesse hält sich ebenso verborgen wie seine Kunstfertigkeit. Und dennoch tritt deutlich zutage – in Bildern wie *Un poco alegre y graciosa* [Ein bißchen heiter und anmutig, S. 71] und *La buena fama durmiendo* [Schlafender guter Ruf, Titelbild] –, daß er sowohl die Fotografie beherrscht, die auf ihren Gegenstand eingeht, wie Cartier-Bresson es tat, als auch jene, die ihn lenkt, wie Meatyard es tat.

L'utilité objective de cette contradiction est explicitée avec clarté dans la citation d'Alvarez Bravo reproduite en introduction à cet essai. Nous nous trouvons, ici, en face non pas d'un artiste naïf, mais d'une vision intentionnellement indigène.

La distinction est significative. Par accumulation, les images faussement simples d'Alvarez Bravo forment une mosaïque, une vaste suite lyrique ou un poème. Le style de ce poète est celui d'une intimité de conversation tranquille, s'abstenant de toute bravura, d'une virtuosité subsumée sous les rythmes d'un dévoilement graduel. Voici donc l'un de ces corpus artistiques qui demande au spectateur d'entrer dans ce que l'un de mes confrères appelle ‹ une bulle de temps ralenti › en l'occurrence, une variété de temps ralenti, baignée de soleil, noyée des ombres puissantes de l'hémisphère sud.

Son habileté technique et sa sophistication avancent masquées. Nous voyons cependant – dans des images comme *Un poco alegre y graciosa* [Assez gai et gracieux, p.71], et de *La buena fama durmiendo* [La Bonne réputation endormie, 1ᵉ de couverture], qu'il est adepte du mode réactif, comme Cartier-Bresson, et du mode directif, comme Metyard. D'autres images (*Los agachados*

[Unpleasant portrait, page 47], *Luz restirada* [Stretched light, page 77] for example) indicate his grasp of the medium's translative capacities – the exploitable differences between what is in front of the lens and what the combination of camera and film will or can be made to register. His sense of formal structure excited Weston, most especially his *Boy urinating*. His recognition of the camera's versatility as a visual means for creating and describing symbolic relationships can be seen in photograph after photograph: *Ángeles en camión* [Angels in truck, page 65], *Niño maya de Tulum* [Mayan boy of Tulum, page 67]. In works such as *Parábola optica* [Optic parable, page 9] he demonstrates that he is fluent enough to create elegant, intricate puns – which James Joyce termed the highest form of language.

In short, his imagery displays highly conscious formal underpinnings. This extends into his approach to the photographic print as well. Virtuoso printmaking as such has never been a main thrust of Alvarez Bravo's work. His images are never so dependent on the print as a vehicle that their poetry is lost in ink reproduction; indeed, I suspect that he has deliberately worked toward an imagery that could convey its essentials even in the form of mediocre

Andere Bilder (zum Beispiel *Los agachados* [Die Sitzenden, S. 15], *Retrato desagradable* [Unangenehmes Porträt, S. 47], *Luz restirada* [Gespanntes Licht, S. 77]) belegen, daß er die interpretativen Möglichkeiten des Mediums gekonnt nutzt. Weston war begeistert von seinem Sinn für formalen Aufbau, am deutlichsten in seinem Bild *Boy urinating*. Ein Foto nach dem anderen belegt seine Fähigkeit zur Darstellung symbolischer Beziehungen: *Ángeles en camión* [Engel auf Lastwagen, S. 65], *Niño maya de Tulum* [Mayajunge aus Tulum, S. 67]. In Arbeiten wie *Parábola optica* [Optische Parabel, S. 9] demonstriert er, daß er sprachgewandt genug ist, elegante, verzwickte Wortspiele zu schaffen – die James Joyce als höchste Form der Sprache bezeichnete.

Kurz, seine Bilder zeugen von einem äußerst bewußten formalen Unterbau. Virtuose Vergrößerungen als solche haben in Alvarez Bravos Schaffen nie eine herausragende Stellung eingenommen. Seine Bilder waren nie so sehr auf den Abzug als Vehikel angewiesen, daß sie ihre Poesie in einer Reproduktion verloren hätten; ich vermute, daß er sogar bewußt auf Bilder hingearbeitet hat, die ihren Kern selbst in Form eines mittelmäßigen Halbtonbildes vermitteln konnten, damit sie sich leicht

[Hommes assises, p. 15], *Retrato desagradable* [Portrait désagréable, p. 47], *Luz restirada* [Lumière étalée, p. 77], par exemple) montrent l'emprise des capacités translatives du médium – la différence exploitable entre ce qui est devant l'objectif et ce que la combinaison de l'appareil et du film permettent d'enregistrer. Son sens de la structure formelle excitait Weston, en particulier son *Boy urinating*. Cette prise en compte de la souplesse de l'appareil photo en tant que moyen visuel de création et de description des relations symboliques s'observe photo après photo : *Ángeles en camión* [Des anges dans un camion, p. 65], *Niño maya de Tulum* [Garçon maya de Tulum, p. 67]. Dans des œuvres comme *Parábola optica* [Parabole optique, p. 9], il démontre qu'il est parfaitement capable de formuler des jeux de mots élégants et complexes, ce que James Joyce con-sidérait comme la plus haute forme du langage.

En bref, ses images affichent des fondements formels totalement cons-cients. La virtuosité du tireur, en tant que telle, n'a jamais été un moteur principal de l'œuvre d'Alvarez Bravo. Ses images ne sont jamais dé-pendantes de leur traitement car leur poésie risque de se perdre lors de la reproduction. En fait, je le

halftone printing, so that it could be readily disseminated and made accessible to its central subjects, the people of Mexico. Yet he is in fact a master craftsman. Whether cast in color or in such monotone forms as silver bromide and palladium prints, Alvarez Bravo's imagery is full of delicate tonal interaction and subtle chiaroscuro. Certainly one of his constant subjects could be said to be the Mexican light itself – an exorbitant light, a light that appears in his images as a living agent, capable of overwhelming with its brutality, caressing with its lavishness and lust for detail, whispering resonantly in the dark shadows of its own absence.

Alvarez Bravo's work also shows a structural kinship with other workers in his medium. There are connections with Aaron Siskind and Brassaï to be found in his studies of walls. Weston, with whom he corresponded at Tina Modotti's instigation, surely affected him. He shares Clarence John Laughlin's fascination with grave-yards. Paul Strand compared him to Eugène Atget in his love of place; the Czechoslovakian surrealist Josef Sudek is another parallel in that regard. To this list I would feel impelled to add Robert Doisneau, Brassaï again (though from a different angle, that of his feel for

verbreiten und dem Volk von Mexiko zugänglich machen ließen. Und doch ist er wahrhaftig ein Meister seines Faches. Ob in Farbe oder als Silberbromid- oder Palladiumabzüge, Alvarez Bravos Bilder sind immer voll zarter Zwischentöne und subtilem Helldunkel. Eines seiner wiederkehrenden Themen ist das mexikanische Licht selbst – ein Licht, das in seinen Fotografien als lebendiges Wesen erscheint, das zugleich brutal und sanft ist und laut in den dunklen Schatten seiner eigenen Abwesenheit wispert.

Alvarez Bravos Werk zeigt eine gewisse strukturelle Verwandtschaft zu anderen Vertretern seines Faches. In seinen Mauerstudien sind Verbindungen zu Aaron Siskind und Brassaï zu finden. Weston, mit dem er auf Anregung von Tina Modotti korrespondierte, hatte sicher einen gewissen Einfluß auf ihn. Mit Clarence John Laughlin teilte er die Faszination für Friedhöfe. Paul Strand verglich ihn in seiner Liebe zu Orten mit Eugène Atget; der tschechoslowakische Surrealist Josef Sudek bildet in dieser Beziehung eine weitere Parallele. Ich sehe mich genötigt, dieser Liste auch Robert Doisneau, nochmals Brassaï (diesmal für sein Gespür für die Dramen des Straßenlebens) und vor allem André Kertész hinzu-

soupçonne d'avoir délibérément travaillé à des images dont le message essentiel était éronné afin d'être facilement diffusées auprès du peuple mexicain. Il n'en est pas moins un remarquable technicien. Que ce soit en couleur ou sous les formes monochromes de tirages aux sels d'argent ou de palladium, ses images sont emplies de jeux tonaux délicats et de subtils clair-obscur. On pourrait dire également que l'un de ses sujets constants est la lumière du Mexique, à la fois vitale et brutale, douce et détaillée, bruissant en résonance dans les ombres sombres de sa propre absence.

L'œuvre d'Alvarez Bravo témoigne également d'une proximité structurelle d'autres acteurs. On peut y trouver des connexions avec Aaron Siskind et Brassaï. Weston, avec lequel il a correspondu à l'instigation de Tina Modotti, l'a sûrement influencé. Il partage la fascination de Clarence John Laughlin pour les cimetières. Paul Strand le compare à Eugène Atget dans son amour du lieu ; le surréaliste tchèque Josef Sudek est un autre parallèle à cet égard. À cette liste, je suis tenté d'ajouter Robert Doisneau, Brassaï (bien que sous un angle différent, celui de l'attachement aux drames minuscules de la vie des rues) ; et par-

Bicicletas en domingo, 1966

the miniature dramas of street life), and most of all André Kertész: all three have in common with Alvarez Bravo a responsiveness to nuances of human gesture and interaction.

Aside from his portraiture, Alvarez Bravo's images of people are quite unlike the posed, stylized studies of a Bruce Davidson or a Paul Strand. Rather, they are swift, sharp glimpses of the physical manifestations of personal identity, outlined with clarity and without cynicism. Though sometimes ambiguous, as such manifestations can be, their duality is not exaggerated by the photographer. Like Doisneau, Brassaï, and Kertész, Alvarez Bravo is able to make the viewer feel fully present at events by his attunement to other people's rhythms. Himself falling in step with the tempos of their lives in the process of making his images, he thereby allows the viewer to stand awhile in someone else's shoes, observant but unobserved. His concentration is on those instants when human beings – usually alone or in small groups – reveal through their bodies something distinctive about their relationship to the earth, to others, or to themselves.

zufügen: Alle drei haben mit Alvarez Bravo eine hohe Sensibilität für menschliche Gesten und Handlungen gemein.

Von seinen Porträtaufnahmen abgesehen, unterscheiden sich Alvarez Bravos Bilder von Menschen erheblich von den gestellten, stilisierten Studien eines Bruce Davidson oder eines Paul Strand. Sie sind vielmehr flüchtige, kurze Augenblicke der körperlichen Manifestation persönlicher Identität, klar und ohne jeden Zynismus skizziert. Obwohl sie manchmal mehrdeutig sind, wie es solche Offenbarungen sein können, übertreibt der Fotograf ihre Doppeldeutigkeit nicht. Ebenso wie Doisneau, Brassaï und Kertész vermittelt auch Alvarez Bravo dem Betrachter, dadurch daß er sich den Rhythmen anderer Menschen anschmiegt, das Gefühl, am Geschehen teilzuhaben. Indem er sich ganz und gar dem jeweiligen Tempo ihres Lebens anpaßt, während er seine Aufnahmen macht, erlaubt er dem Betrachter, ein Weilchen in die Haut eines anderen zu schlüpfen, beobachtend, aber nicht beobachtet. Er konzentriert sich auf jene Momente, in denen Menschen – meist allein oder in kleinen Gruppen – durch ihren Körper etwas über ihre Beziehung zur Erde, zu anderen oder zu sich selbst deutlich enthüllen.

dessus tout, André Kertész : tous trois ont en commun avec Alvarez Bravo une sympathie pour les infinies nuances de la geste humaine et des rapports entre les hommes.

En dehors des portraits, les images d'individus d'Alvarez Bravo sont assez différentes des études posées et stylisées d'un Bruce Davidson ou d'un Paul Strand. Ce sont plutôt des coups d'œil vifs et aigus sur les manifestations physiques d'une identité personnelle, soulignées avec clarté et sans cynisme. Bien que parfois ambiguës, comme peuvent l'être de telles expressions, leur dualité n'est pas exagérée par le photographe. Comme Doisneau, Brassaï et Kertész, Alvarez Bravo sait rendre le spectateur entièrement présent à l'événement représenté en se mettant pleinement à l'écoute des autres. Se mettant lui-même en rythme avec les *tempi* de leur vie lors de la fabrication de ses images, il permet du même coup au spectateur de se mettre dans les pas de l'autre. Sa concentration se fait sur ces instants où les êtres humains – habituellement seuls ou en petit groupe – révèlent à travers leur corps un fait remarquable dans leur relation avec la terre, les autres ou avec eux-mêmes.

Árbol que partió un rayo, 1956

Alvarez Bravo is anything but unaware of art forms outside his own. He is an authority on Mexican mural art (which he has photographed officially for many years). His peers are the modern masters – Diego Rivera, José Clemente Orozco, David Alfaro Siqueiros, et al. – who often posed for him. His work has long been known to the surrealists, and he has surely learned from them in turn. (Witness his use of titles that do not merely reiterate the image contents but instead specify and/or extend their metaphorical implications: *Trampa puesta* [Placed trap, page 87], *Paisaje y galope* [Landscape and gallop, page 13], *Retrato póstumo* [Posthumous portrait, page 69], for example.)

Yet the major force which has shaped his imagery has not been art, but culture. The themes around which his work revolves are quintessentially Mexican, motifs so traditional as to be more unavoidable than chosen. What are his predilections? Dogs and dreams, ladders and walls, birds, people, earth, and death.

Given a body of work as extensive and interrelated as Alvarez Bravo's, it is difficult to single out individual images for examination. Ideally, one should be able to refer the reader to a wide, representative crosssection.

Alvarez Bravo ist sich der Kunstformen außerhalb seines Faches durchaus bewußt. Er ist eine Autorität auf dem Gebiet mexikanischer Wandmalereien (die er jahrelang offiziell fotografiert hat). Ihm ebenbürtige moderne Meister wie Diego Rivera, José Clemente Orozco, David Alfaro Siqueiros und andere saßen ihm oft Modell. Den Surrealisten waren seine Arbeiten seit langem bekannt, und er hat seinerseits sicher von ihnen gelernt. (Man beachte seine Bildtitel, die nicht nur den Bildinhalt wiedergeben, sondern die metaphorischen Implikationen spezifizieren und/oder erweitern: zum Beispiel *Trampa puesta* [Gestellte Falle, S. 87], *Paisaje y galope* [Landschaft und Galopp, S. 13], *Retrato póstumo* [Posthumes Porträt, S. 69].)

Die wichtigste Kraft, die seine Fotografien prägt, ist jedoch nicht die Kunst, sondern die Kultur. Die Themen, um die sein Schaffen sich dreht, sind ihrem Wesen nach mexikanisch, Motive, die so traditionell sind, daß sie nicht selbst gewählt wirken. Welche Vorlieben hat er? Hunde und Träume, Leitern und Wände, Vögel, Menschen, die Erde und den Tod.

Angesichts eines so umfassenden und verflochtenen Gesamtwerks, wie Alvarez Bravo es geschaffen hat, fällt es schwer, einzelne Bilder für eine

Alvarez Bravo est parfaitement conscient des formes d'art autres que la sienne. Il est une autorité en matière d'art mural mexicain (dont il a été le photographe officiel pendant des années). Ses pairs sont les maîtres modernes – Diego Rivera, José Clemente Orozco, David Alfaro Siqueiros, et d'autres – qui ont souvent posé pour lui. Son travail est connu depuis longtemps par les Surréalistes, et il a certainement beaucoup appris d'eux (comme le prouve son usage de titres qui ne décrivent pas seulement le contenu de l'image, mais spécifie et/ ou étendent leurs implications métaphoriques : *Trampa puesta* [Le piège posé, p. 87], *Paisaje y galope* [Paysage au galop, p. 13], *Retrato póstumo* [Portrait posthume, p. 69], par exemple.

Cependant, la force principale qui lui a permis de mettre en forme son œuvre n'est pas l'art, mais la culture. Les thèmes autour desquels il travaille sont quintessentiellement mexicains, motifs traditionnels plus inévitables que choisis. Quelles sont ses prédilections ? Les chiens et les rêves, les échelles et les murs, les oiseaux, les gens, la terre, la mort.

Face à une œuvre aussi étendue et intriquée que celle d'Alvarez Bravo, il est difficile d'examiner une seule image. Idéalement, on devrait pou-

This is only now becoming possible, thanks in part to the present volume, a few of its predecessors (unfortunately out of print), and a surge of recent one-person exhibitions[2]. Let me, then, discuss a few images for what they might suggest of the whole.

I begin with one of a man lying face upward on the earth. From the sheer volume of blood which has poured out of his mouth and nose to spatter his clothing, pool under his head, and soak into the soil, I would assume that he is dead. However, the small sharp gleam of light in the corner of his left eye suggests in a most disconcerting way that his life continues. The cause of death is not apparent; it may have been external violence or internal hemorrhage. He seems at rest; his body is stretched out, his expression is not fearful or contorted. The photograph brings the viewer close to him, close enough to study his profile and note the details of his clothing – but not so close as to cut him off above the groin or to amputate his slightly curled left hand.

genauere Betrachtung auszuwählen. Idealerweise müßte man den Leser auf einen repräsentativen Querschnitt verweisen. Dies ist erst jetzt möglich, dank des vorliegenden Bandes, einiger seiner (leider vergriffenen) Vorläufer und einer Flut von Einzelausstellungen in letzter Zeit[2]. Im folgenden bespreche ich ausführlicher einige für Alvarez Bravos Gesamtwerk repräsentative Bilder.

Beginnen möchte ich mit einem Bild, auf dem ein Mann mit dem Gesicht nach oben auf der Erde liegt. Aus der Menge des Blutes, das ihm aus Mund und Nase geflossen ist, seine Kleider befleckt, eine Lache unter seinem Kopf gebildet hat und in die Erde gesickert ist, würde ich schließen, daß er tot ist. Der winzige Lichtfunke im linken Augenwinkel deutet jedoch auf äußerst verwirrende Weise an, daß sein Leben weitergeht. Die Todesursache ist nicht erkennbar. Er wirkt friedlich; sein Körper ist ausgestreckt, seine Miene weder angsterfüllt noch verzerrt. Die Fotografie bringt den Betrachter ihm nahe, nah genug, sein Profil und Details seiner Kleidung zu erkennen – aber nicht so nah, daß sie seine Hüften oder seine leicht gekrümmte linke Hand abschneiden würde.

voir renvoyer le lecteur à un choix large et représentatif. Ceci commence seulement à être possible aujourd'hui, grâce en partie à cet ouvrage, à certains de ses prédécesseurs (malheureusement épuisés) et à une multiplication récente d'expositions personnelles[2]. Nous pouvons néanmoins analyser quelques images pour mieux comprendre leur ensemble.

Je commencerai par celle d'un homme qui gît sur le sol, visage vers le ciel. De l'effrayant volume de sang qui s'est échappé de sa bouche et de son nez pour se répandre sur ses vêtements, de la flaque sous sa tête, et de la terre qui en est imbibée, je présume qu'il est mort. Cependant, un mince rayon de lumière au coin de son œil gauche suggère d'une façon déconcertante que la vie continue peut-être. La cause de la mort n'est pas connue. Il semble au repos. Son corps est détendu, son expression n'est ni apeurée ni tourmentée. La photographie nous rapproche de lui, assez près pour que nous puissions étudier son profil et les détails de ses vêtements – mais il est néanmoins cadré au niveau de l'entrejambes et de sa main gauche légèrement refermée.

Violín Huichol, 1965

Aside from the man himself, his blood, and the earth, there are no other contents in the image, except for some dim folds of cloth in the background and the hint of another's hand or foot in the upper left corner. Instead of making his image at more of a distance (thus distancing the viewer equally from the event), or portraying the body in relation to other people at the scene (giving it more of a public quality), or looking down from above the body (with the overtones of superiority/triumph that would add), the photographer's choice of position places the viewer at the dead man's left side, the side closest to his heart, inches from his hand, crouching or kneeling – the place of a doctor, a friend or relative, a mourner.

I have always felt a powerful upward thrust in this image, as though the prone body were on the verge of rising horizontally from the ground. With the image turned on its side so that his head is at the top, the man seems quite alive and intent, his body rushing forward into space like Mercury's. Perhaps this response has to do with the counterpoised diagonals of the image's structure, or with the almost aerodynamic flow of his hair and blood.

Außer diesem Mann, seinem Blut und der Erde gibt es keinen anderen Bildinhalt, abgesehen von den vagen Falten eines Stoffes und der Andeutung einer Hand oder eines Fußes von jemand anderem in der oberen linken Ecke. Statt sein Foto aus größerer Entfernung aufzunehmen (und damit den Betrachter zugleich auf Distanz zum Geschehen zu bringen) oder den Körper in Beziehung zu anderen Menschen am Schauplatz zu setzen (was ihm einen öffentlicheren Charakter verliehen hätte) oder von oben auf den Körper herabzuschauen (wodurch ein Gefühl der Überlegenheit vermittelt würde), versetzt die vom Fotografen gewählte Position den Betrachter hockend oder kniend an die linke Seite des Mannes, der Seite seines Herzens – so nimmt der Betrachtende den Platz eines Arztes, Freundes, Verwandten oder Trauernden ein.

Ich habe in diesem Bild immer einen starken Zug nach oben verspürt, als sei der flach ausgestreckte Körper im Begriff, sich horizontal vom Boden zu erheben. Dreht man das Bild auf die Seite, so daß der Kopf oben ist, dann wirkt der Mann recht lebendig und entschlossen. Vielleicht hat dieser Eindruck etwas mit den gegenläufigen Diagonalen des Bildaufbaus zu tun oder mit dem Fließenden seiner Haare und des Blutes.

Hormis l'homme lui-même, son sang, le sol, quelques plis d'une étoffe et la main ou le pied de quelqu'un d'autre dans le coin supérieur gauche, l'image ne contient rien d'autre. Au lieu de nous présenter cette image prise de plus loin (distançant ainsi le spectateur de l'événement), ou de prendre le corps avec d'autres personnes présentes sur les lieux (lui conférant une qualité plus publique), ou en plongée (avec les connotations de supériorité que cela pourrait ajouter), le photographe a choisi une position qui place l'observateur, s'agenouillant à la gauche du mort, du côté du cœur. Comme un médecin, un ami ou un parent, un pleureur.

J'ai toujours ressenti un puissant sentiment d'élévation dans cette image, comme si le corps couché était sur le point de s'élever horizontalement au-dessus du sol. Si l'on tourne l'image sur le côté de façon à placer la tête en haut, l'homme semble presque vivant et déterminé. Cette impression tient peut-être aux diagonales opposées qui structurent l'image, ou au flux presque aérodynamique de sa chevelure et de son sang.

El soñador, 1931

So, by itself, the image suggests the unexpected death of a seemingly average young man, a death accepted with a certain equanimity; it indicates the cyclical inevitability of the body's return to the dust by depicting that quite literally; it accepts that cycle of the flesh stoically. Yet the vitality of the figure and of the image itself implies some transcendence of the spirit. By itself, we might think of this image as a memorial.

But the image has a title: *Obrero en huelga, asesinado* [Striking worker, assassinated, page 59]. The title is strictly – and, for Alvarez Bravo, rigorously – informational. The information it offers us could not be deduced from the image. We might have guessed that the man was a worker; we could not have known that he was on strike, nor surely that the cause of his death was political, not accidental. Yet this title does not contradict the impression of the image; instead it elaborates it by providing the context in which to ponder this particular death, a context in which the symbolism of the image echoes, reverberates, expands. From the combination of the two – the visual data in the image, the verbal data of the caption – we are free to write out our own equations.

Das Foto zeigt also den unerwarteten Tod eines offenbar durchschnittlichen jungen Mannes, einen Tod, der mit einem gewissen Gleichmut akzeptiert wird; es zeugt von der unausweichlichen Rückkehr des Körpers zu Staub, indem es sie bildlich darstellt; der Zyklus des Fleisches wird scheinbar akzeptiert. Doch die Lebendigkeit der Gestalt und des Bildes selbst verweist auf eine gewisse Transzendenz des Geistes. Dieses Bild läßt sich als Mahnmal interpretieren.

Das Bild hat jedoch einen Titel: *Obrero en huelga, asesinado* [Streikender Arbeiter, ermordet, S. 59]. Die Information, die er uns gibt, läßt sich aus dem Bild nicht ableiten. Daß der Mann Arbeiter war, hätten wir noch erraten können; daß er sich im Streik befand, konnten wir jedoch nicht wissen, noch weniger, daß seine Todesursache eine politische war und kein Unfall. Der Titel widerspricht dem Eindruck des Bildes jedoch nicht, sondern er verstärkt ihn noch, indem er diesen speziellen Tod in einen Kontext stellt, so daß der Symbolcharakter des Bildes widerhallt, nachhallt, sich ausdehnt. Ausgehend von der Kombination von Bild und Text bleibt es uns freigestellt, unsere eigenen Schlüsse zu ziehen.

Ainsi l'image suggère-t-elle la mort inattendue d'un jeune homme apparemment sans qualités particulières, un mort accepté avec une certaine sérénité. Elle montre l'inévitabilité du retour du corps à la poussière en décrivant le phénomène de manière quasi littérale. Elle accepte stoïquement le cycle de la chair. Cependant la vitalité du personnage et de l'image elle-même implique une certaine transcendance de l'esprit. Nous pourrions penser qu'il s'agit d'un mémorial.

Mais l'image a un titre : *Obrero en huelga, asesinado* [Travailleur en grève assassiné, p. 59]. Le titre est purement informatif. L'information qu'il nous offre ne pourrait être déduite de l'image. Nous aurions pu deviner que l'homme était un ouvrier ; nous ne pouvions pas savoir qu'il était en grève, ni davantage que la cause de sa mort était politique, et non accidentelle. Ce titre ne contredit pas pour autant l'impression de l'image. Il l'approfondit en nous fournissant le contexte dans lequel la valeur de cette mort se précise, contexte dans lequel le symbolisme de l'image fait écho, reflète et se développe. De la combinaison des deux – la donnée visuelle de l'image, et la donnée verbale de la légende – nous sommes libres de composer notre propre équation.

Tumba reciente, 1939

Though it was never intended to function photojournalistically, this particular image is, in the context of this body of work, untypically topical – almost an hommage to the great documentarian of the Mexican Revolution, Augustin Casasola. However, this is only one of many images by Alvarez Bravo in which death is the central issue. His work is full of tombs, cemeteries, coffins, the cadavers and skeletons of various creatures, and the religious/ceremonial artifacts with which mortality is celebrated in Mexico. If mortality – seen as the return to dust – is central to Alvarez Bravo's art, then this image is surely the epicenter, the one which brings him (and us) closest to the moment of transition from life to death. From it radiates outward much of his imagery: the diverse visions of death; people and animals lying on the ground, drawing sustenance from their soil in order to nourish it in turn; people laboring on or in the dirt, always in contact with it.

The photographer offers no escape from that connection. Walls pretend to divide and control the earth, but they continually crumble – reminding us of their earthly origin – or diminish the human protagonist. Ladders offer a way of climbing, but only for a time: they are always

Obwohl diese Aufnahme nie als Beitrag zum Fotojournalismus gedacht war, ist sie im Kontext des Gesamtwerks von einer für Bravo nicht typischen Aktualität – fast eine Hommage an den großen Chronisten der Mexikanischen Revolution Augustin Casasola. Dies ist jedoch nur ein Bild unter vielen, in denen Alvarez Bravo den Tod zum zentralen Thema macht. In seinem Werk kommen viele Gräber, Friedhöfe, Särge, Kadaver und Skelette verschiedener Kreaturen und die religiös-zeremoniellen Artefakte vor, mit denen man in Mexiko der Sterblichkeit gedenkt. Wenn Sterblichkeit – als Rückkehr zu Staub verstanden – eine zentrale Stellung in Alvarez Bravos Schaffen einnimmt, ist dieses Bild sicher das Epizentrum, das ihn (und uns) jenem Augenblick des Übergangs vom Leben zum Tod am nächsten bringt. Von dieser Aufnahme leitet sich ein Großteil seiner Bilder ab: die diversen Sichtweisen des Todes; Menschen und Tiere, die am Boden liegen und ihre Nahrung aus der Erde ziehen, um sie wiederum zu nähren; Menschen, die auf oder im Staub arbeiten, in ständigem Kontakt mit ihm.

Aus dieser Verbindung bietet der Fotograf keinen Ausweg an. Mauern geben vor, die Erde zu teilen oder zu kontrollieren, aber sie bröckeln

Bien qu'elle n'ait jamais eu l'intention de fonctionner comme un document photojournalistique, cette image particulière est – dans le contexte de cette œuvre atypiquement allusive – presque un hommage au grand documentaliste de la Révolution Mexicaine, Augustin Casasola. Il ne s'agit cependant que de l'une des nombreuses images d'Alvarez Bravo dans laquelle la mort est le sujet principal. Son œuvre est emplie de tombes, de cimetières, de cercueils, de cadavres et de squelettes de diverses créatures, et des artefacts religieux et de cérémonie qui entourent le décès au Mexique. Si la mort – vue comme un retour à la poussière – occupe une place centrale dans l'art d'Alvarez Bravo, cette image en est alors certainement l'épicentre. De cette image irradie l'un des grands thèmes de son œuvre : visions diverses de la mort, d'êtres humains et d'animaux couchés sur le sol, tirant leur substance de leur terre avant de la nourrir en retour, de gens qui travaillent sur ou dans la poussière, toujours en contact avec elle.

Le photographe n'offre aucune sortie de secours à cette connexion. Les murs prétendent diviser et contrôler le sol, ici ils s'effondrent continuellement – en rappelant leur origine terrienne – ou réduisent la

Las espinas, c1940

connected to the earth, often at more than one end, as is indicated in the ironic *Ladders of ladders,* 1931, in which a ladder leads upward to a child-sized coffin on a shelf. Only birds get to leave the earth, and even they are eventually snared to death (as in *Twilight bird swayed by the wind,* 1932), brought down at last.

If there is no escape, there is at least one release: dreaming. It is another recurrent motif in Alvarez Bravo's work: *Quevedo* [Dreams are for believing], 1968, *Dogs bark while sleeping,* 1966, *Good reputation sleeping,* 1938, *The day dream,* 1931[3], are a few of the images in which it figures. But we might use *El soñador* [The dreamer, 1931, page 29], as an exemplification, if only because it dovetails so precisely with *Obrero en huelga, asesinado.*

In this image also a man lies face upward on the earth. There is grass around his head and feet, but he appears to be on top of a ledge, or perhaps the uppermost of several

unablässig und erinnern uns an ihren irdischen Ursprung oder machen den menschlichen Protagonisten klein. Leitern bieten eine Möglichkeit zu klettern, aber nur vorübergehend: Immer sind sie mit der Erde verbunden, oft mit mehr als nur einem Ende, wie es das ironische Bild *Ladders of ladders,* 1931, zeigt, auf dem eine Leiter nach oben führt, zu einem Kindersarg auf einem Regal. Nur Vögeln gelingt es, sich von der Erde zu lösen, und selbst sie werden schließlich vom Tod umfangen (wie in *Twilight bird swayed by the wind,* 1932) und niedergestreckt.

Wenn es schon keinen Ausweg gibt, so gibt es doch eine Befreiung: das Träumen – ein weiteres immer wiederkehrendes Motiv in Alvarez Bravos Werk: *Quevedo* [Träume sind zum Glauben da], 1968; *Dogs bark while sleeping,* 1966; *Good reputation sleeping,* 1938; *The day dream,* 1931[3], um nur einige Bilder zu nennen, in denen es vorkommt. Als Beispiel könnten wir *El soñador* [Der Träumer, 1931, S. 29], nehmen, und sei es auch nur, weil es haargenau zu *Obrero en huelga, asesinado* paßt.

Auch hier liegt ein Mann mit dem Gesicht nach oben auf dem Boden. Um Kopf und Füße wächst Gras, aber es sieht aus, als läge er auf einem Sims

taille du protagoniste humain. Les échelles offrent une façon de grimper, mais sont toujours connectées à la terre, parfois aux deux extrémités comme dans l'ironique *Ladders of ladders* (1931), dans laquelle une échelle mène à un cercueil d'enfant placé sur une étagère. Seuls les oiseaux ont la possibilité de quitter cette terre, même s'ils sont eux aussi parfois dominés par la mort (comme dans *Twilight bird swayed by the wind,* 1932).

S'il n'y a pas de sortie de secours, il y au moins une échappatoire : le rêve. C'est un autre des motifs récurrents de l'œuvre d'Alvarez Bravo, illustré, entre autres, par *Quevedo,* 1968, *Dogs bark while sleeping,* 1966, *Good reputation sleeping,* 1938, *The day dream,* 1931[3]. Mais nous pouvons faire de *El soñador,* [Le Rêveur, 1931, p. 29], une exemplification, ne serait-ce que par ce qu'il rejoint précisément *Obrero en huelga, asesinado.*

Dans cette image, un homme est étendu sur le sol, face vers le ciel. Il y a de l'herbe au dessus de sa tête et des ses pieds, mais il semble se tenir en haut d'un rebord, ou peut-être au sommet d'une volée de marches de

Magueyes heridos, 1950

stone steps. He is lying on his right side. In many ways he resembles the striking worker: for if he is unshaven and poor, he is also at rest, facing the sky, hair flowing back to touch the ground. They even look somewhat alike: about the same age and size.

Through the camera we are positioned on the same level as the dreamer – or, rather, he being at our eye level, somewhat below him. We are also somewhat farther back from him than we were from the worker; the difference is no more than a foot or two, but it is enough to show him full length and also enough to insulate his reverie from the intrusion of camera and photographer.

Unlike the worker, who stares with open eyes into a harsh, flat light, the dreamer's eyes are closed and brushed, like much of his body, with a gentle, mellow glow of sun. Perhaps it warms him enough to make him dream of making love; perhaps that is why his left hand (again, unlike the worker's) is tucked between his closed legs, pressed against his sex. It is that possibility, at least, which Alvarez Bravo asks us to consider.

oder auf der obersten Stufe einer Steintreppe. Er liegt auf der rechten Seite. In mancher Hinsicht hat er Ähnlichkeit mit dem streikenden Arbeiter: Er ist zwar unrasiert und arm, aber voller Ruhe, hat das Gesicht gen Himmel gewandt, und sein Haar fällt fließend nach hinten und berührt die Erde. Sie sehen sich sogar ein bißchen ähnlich.

Die Kamera stellt uns auf eine Ebene mit dem Träumer – oder vielmehr, er ist fast für uns auf Augenhöhe. Wir sind von ihm auch etwas weiter entfernt als von dem Arbeiter; es handelt sich um eine Distanz von ein bis zwei Schritten, die aber genügt, ihn in voller Körpergröße zu zeigen und seine Träumerei vor dem Eindringen der Kamera und des Fotografen zu schützen.

Anders als der Arbeiter, der mit offenen Augen in ein harsches, kontrastarmes Licht starrt, hat der Träumer die Augen geschlossen, und sein Körper ist in ein sanftes Sonnenlicht gehüllt. Vielleicht läßt es ihn von der Liebe träumen; vielleicht hat er deshalb die linke Hand (wieder anders als der Arbeiter) zwischen den geschlossenen Beinen, fest an seinem Geschlecht. Zumindest fordert Alvarez Bravo uns auf, diese Möglichkeit in Betracht zu ziehen.

pierre. Il est étendu sur son côté droit. Il ressemble de multiples façons à l'ouvrier en grève : mal rasé et pauvre, il est lui aussi au repos, visage regardant le ciel, chevelure rejetée en arrière touchant le sol. Ils ont presque l'air identique.

À travers l'appareil photo, nous nous trouvons au même niveau que le rêveur, ou plutôt, il se trouve à celui de nos yeux, un peu en-dessous. Nous sommes également un peu plus éloigné que dans l'image de l'ouvrier. La différence n'est que de quelques dizaines de centimètres, ce qui suffit pour le montrer à pleine taille, et protéger sa rêverie de l'intrusion de l'appareil et du photographe.

À la différence de l'ouvrier, qui regarde les yeux ouverts vers une lumière dure et plate, ceux du rêveur sont fermés, baignés de l'éclat tendre et doux du soleil. Peut-être le laisse-t-il rêver à l'amour ; peut-être est-ce la raison pour laquelle sa main gauche (à la différence de celle de l'ouvrier) est calée entre ses jambes serrées, pressée contre son sexe. C'est cette possibilité qu'Alvarez Bravo nous incite à considérer.

Xipe, la segunda, 1982

So they are different, the worker and the dreamer; and yet they are alike. I think it is important to recognize that Alvarez Bravo acknowledges both these realities in his work. Each person he portrays is an individual, and the photographer gives to each one his or her personal identity through his attunement to the subtleties of gesture, posture, and expression. Yet they resemble each other, bound together by their indigence and their share in an ancient culture.

The photographer's sense of the complexity of this issue is summed up in another image. It portrays two men at work on a beach. They stand face to face, the one on the left reaching for a basket of sand on the head of the other. Were it not for that difference in gesture, they could be mirror images of each other: their hats, their short pants, their bodies, their stances are identical. One can imagine them as twin brothers, or children who grew up together as friends in the same community, under the same circumstances, and who have grown so like each other from being polished to an identical smoothness by the same shared experiences. It seems unlikely that they could come to differ radically from each other, that their lives could

So unterschiedlich der Arbeiter und der Träumer sind, so sehr ähneln sie sich aber auch. Ich halte es für wichtig festzustellen, daß Alvarez Bravo diese beiden Realitäten in seinem Werk einfängt. Er räumt jeder Person ihre eigene Identität ein, indem er sich auf die Feinheiten der Geste, der Haltung und des Ausdrucks einstellt. Und doch ähneln sie sich, verbunden durch ihre Herkunft und ihren Anteil an einer alten Kultur.

Das Gespür des Fotografen für die Komplexität dieses Aspekts ist in einem anderen Bild zusammengefaßt. Es zeigt zwei Männer bei der Arbeit am Strand. Sie stehen sich gegenüber, der linke greift nach einem Korb Sand auf dem Kopf des anderen. Abgesehen von diesem Unterschied in den Gesten sind sie völlig identisch. Man kann sich vorstellen, daß sie Zwillinge oder Freunde sind, die sich, geprägt durch die gleichen, gemeinsamen Erfahrungen, so ähnlich geworden sind. Es erscheint unwahrscheinlich, daß sie sich je radikal unterscheiden könnten, daß ihr Leben sich je ändern könnte. Und doch vollführen sie dieses ewige Sisyphosritual mit der Sicherheit und der Grazie von Solotänzern. Alvarez Bravo nennt sie *Los mismos* [Die Gleichen].

Ainsi l'ouvrier et le rêveur sont différents et en même temps semblables, et Alvarez Bravo prend en compte ces deux réalités dans son travail. Il donne à chaque personne qu'il photographie son identité en se soumettant aux subtilités des gestes, des postures et des expressions. Et pourtant ils se ressemblent par leur indigence et leur appartenance à une ancienne culture.

Chez le photographe, le sens de la complexité de cet enjeu est résumé dans une autre image. Elle représente deux hommes au travail sur une plage. Ils sont face à face, celui de gauche prenant un panier de sable sur la tête de l'autre. Sans cette différence de geste, chacun pourrait être pris pour le reflet de l'autre. On pourrait les imaginer en jumeaux, ou en enfants qui ont grandi ensemble dans la même communauté, dans les mêmes circonstances, et qui ont poussé de manière identique, polis avec la même douceur par le partage d'une même existence. Il semble improbable qu'ils aient pu être différents, que leurs vies puissent changer. Et ils interprètent ce rituel éternel de Sisyphe avec l'assurance et la grâce de danseurs. Alvarez Bravo, les a intitulés *Los mismos* [Les Mêmes].

ever change. Yet they enact this eternal Sisyphean ritual with the assurance and grace of solo dancers. Alvarez Bravo names them *Los mismos* [The same].

Immersed in culture, yet devoid of sentimentality, Alvarez Bravo requires that his work has emotional and intellectual accessibilty as well as formal logic, continuity, and growth. His imagery may be fugitive, but it is not secretive. Though he speaks in the vernacular with eloquence, his perceptions inevitably transcend what Latin American critics have termed, disparagingly, the merely "folkloric." There is little of the specifically autobiographical in Alvarez Bravo's photographs; instead, their authenticity springs from intuitions and understandings of his themes whose basis is an embrace of cultural experience. He is a paradigm of the rare, invaluable photographer who chooses to serve as the eye of his people – and who, by probing into the heart of his own culture so as to bear witness to its vitality, exposes something of the essence of all human experience.

Despite his single-minded focus on his homeland, there is nothing either anthropological or parochial in his approach. At once ironic and emotional, sympathetic yet detached,

Eingebettet in seine Kultur, aber ohne jede Sentimentalität verlangt Alvarez Bravo von seinem Werk, daß es emotional und intellektuell zugänglich ist und zugleich formale Logik, Kontinuität und Entwicklung besitzt. Seine Bilder mögen flüchtig sein, verschlossen sind sie jedoch nicht. Obwohl er die Sprache des Volkes spricht, geht seine Wahrnehmung unausweichlich über das hinaus, was Lateinamerikakritiker verzweifelt als das rein »Folkloristische« bezeichnet haben. Alvarez Bravos Fotografien haben wenig Autobiographisches; sie beziehen ihre Authentizität aus dem Verständnis für seine Themen, die sich auf kulturelle Erfahrung stützen. Das ist das Paradigma jenes wertvollen Fotografen, der als Auge seines Volkes dient – und der, indem er ins Herz seiner eigenen Kultur eindringt, um Zeugnis von ihrer Lebendigkeit abzulegen, etwas vom Kern allen menschlichen Erlebens offenlegt.

Obwohl er sich voll und ganz seinem Heimatland gewidmet hat, geht seine Herangehensweise über einen beschränkten Raum hinaus. Alvarez Bravos Weltsicht, gleichermaßen ironisch wie emotional, mitfühlend wie distanziert, umwirbt, bil- ligt und akzeptiert aktiv und begierig die Widersprüche und Komplexitäten

Immergé dans la culture, mais dénué de tout sentimentalisme, Alvarez Bravo donne à son œuvre une accessibilité émotionnelle et intellectuelle, en même temps qu'une logique formelle, une continuité, une pulsion. Ses images peuvent être surprises, mais n'ont rien de secret. Bien qu'il parle le langage de la rue avec éloquence, ses perceptions transcendent inévitablement ce que les critiques latino-américains ont qualifié, de manière désobligeante, de tout au plus « folklorique ». Il n'y a pas grand chose d'autobiographique dans les photographies d'Alvarez Bravo. Leur authenticité jaillit bien plutôt d'intuitions et de compréhension de ces thèmes dont la base est fondée sur l'expérience culturelle. Il est le paradigme du photographe rare, inestimable, qui choisit d'être l'œil de son peuple, et qui en sondant le cœur de sa propre culture afin de se porter témoin de sa vitalité, expose quelque chose de l'essence de l'existence de l'homme.

Bien qu'il se soit exclusivement consacré à son pays natal, il n'y a rien d'anthropologique ou de local dans son approche. Ironique et sensible, sympathique mais détaché, l'univers d'Alvarez Bravo observe activement et sollicite ardemment, avalise et enveloppe les contradictions et les

Alvarez Bravo's world view actively and eagerly courts, endorses, and encompasses the contradictions and complexities of the culture to which it is symbiotically bound. If it were possible to restore dignity to the term 'ethnocentric,' then I would apply that word to his body of work – for it accepts Mexico and its people as a viable and sufficient metaphor for life itself.

Such an acceptance – far from uncritical, but equally far from cynicism and alienation – is the source of his work's integrity and power. His work makes no plea, sounds no alarms over transient plights, and polemicizes no issues. The people of Manuel Alvarez Bravo's images bear as their birthright (often their only one) the knowledge that they will feed their native land with their toil and their flesh as their ancestors have done back into pre-history.[4] That is their burden, and their badge. Despite what economics may indicate, no matter what politicians and business-men and the military may enforce, the land – and the culture – is theirs. Death is the equalizer.

But life is a dream.

A.D. Coleman
New York City

ten der Kultur, mit der er verbunden ist. Wenn es möglich wäre, den Begriff ›ethnozentrisch‹ wieder mit Würde auszustatten, würde ich ihn auf sein Gesamtwerk anwenden – denn es akzeptiert Mexiko und sein Volk als lebendige und hinreichende Metapher für das Leben an sich.

Dieses Akzeptieren – weit davon entfernt, unkritisch zu sein, aber ebenso weit entfernt von Zynismus und Entfremdung – ist die Quelle für die Kraft seines Werkes. Es hält kein Plädoyer, schlägt nicht Alarm wegen vergänglicher Miseren und polemisiert nicht. Die Menschen in Manuel Alvarez Bravos Bildern sind von Geburt an mit dem Wissen ausgestattet (und das ist ihr einziger Besitz), daß sie ihre Heimat mit ihrer mühseligen Arbeit und ihrem Fleisch ernähren werden wie ihre Vorfahren es seit Urzeiten getan haben[4]. Das ist ihre Bürde und ihre Auszeichnung. Was immer auch Politiker, Geschäftsleute und Militärs durchsetzen mögen, das Land – und die Kultur – gehört ihnen. Der Tod ist der Gleichmacher.

Und das Leben ist ein Traum.

A.D. Coleman
New York City

complexités d'une culture à laquelle il est symbiotiquement lié. S'il était possible de redonner une dignité au terme ‹ ethnocentrique ›, j'aimerais l'appliquer à ce travail, qui accepte le Mexique et son peuple comme une métaphore viable et suffisante de la vie elle-même.

Une telle acceptation – loin d'être une critique, mais tout aussi loin du cynisme ou de l'aliénation – est la source de l'intégrité et de la puissance de cette œuvre. Elle ne fait pas de procès, n'alarme pas sur les problèmes quotidiens, ni ne lance de polémique. Le peuple des images d'Alvarez Bravo porte comme une marque de naissance (souvent la seule) la connaissance qu'il nourrira sa terre de sa chair et de son travail comme ses ancêtres le font depuis avant l'histoire[4]. C'est leur distinction. En dépit de ce que les économistes diront, et de ce que feront les politiciens, les hommes d'affaires et les militaires, c'est son fardeau et sa marque personnelle. La mort est la grande égalisatrice.

Mais la vie est un rêve.

A. D. Coleman
New York City

NOTES

This essay is an updated and expanded version of one that originally appeared in *Artforum,* April 1976 and was reprinted in A.D. Coleman, *Light Readings,* New York: Oxford University Press, 1978.

1. Emily Edwards, *Painted Walls of Mexico: From Prehistoric Times until Today,* photographs by Manuel Alvarez Bravo, Austin: University of Texas Press, 1968, p. 145.

2. Although out of print, see, for example, Jane Livingston, *M. Alvarez Bravo,* Boston and Washington, DC: David R. Godine and the Corcoran Gallery of Art, 1978, and *Manuel Alvarez Bravo: fotografias 1928-1968,* text by Juan Garcia Ponce, Mexico: Instituto Nacional de Bellas Artes, D.F.: Comite Organizador de Los Juegos de Las XIX Olimpiada, 1968. Retrospectives have been held during the past several years at the International Center of Photography in New York and the Musée d'Art Moderne de la Ville de Paris, with a catalog of the 303-print exhibition, *Manuel Alvarez Bravo: 1920-1986,* Paris: Paris Musées/Paris Audio Visuel, 1986.

3. This particular image has a historical forbear in O.G. Rejlander's *The Bachelor's Dream,* and at least one offspring in the third image from the last in Ralph Gibson's *Déjà-Vu.*

4. Alvarez Bravo's own connection with the same land pervades his images.

ANMERKUNGEN

Bei diesem Beitrag handelt es sich um die aktualisierte und erweiterte Fassung eines Essays, das ursprünglich in *Artforum,* April 1976, erschienen ist und in A.D. Coleman, *Light Readings,* New York, Oxford University Press, 1978, aufgenommen wurde.

1. Emily Edwards, *Painted Walls of Mexico: From Prehistoric Times until Today,* Fotografien von Manuel Alvarez Bravo, Austin, University of Texas Press, 1968, S. 145.

2. Siehe zum Beispiel den leider vergriffenen Titel von Jane Livingston, *M. Alvarez Bravo,* Boston und Washington, DC, David R. Godine und die Corcoran Gallery of Art, 1978; und *Manuel Alvarez Bravo: fotografias 1928–1968,* Text: Juan Garcia Ponce, Mexiko, Instituto Nacional de Bellas Artes, D.F.: Comite Organizador de Los Juegos de Las XIX Olimpiada, 1968. In den letzten Jahren fanden Retrospektiven im International Center of Photography, New York, und im Musée d'Art Moderne de la Ville de Paris statt; zu der Pariser Ausstellung mit 303 Fotografien ist ein Katalog erschienen: *Manuel Alvarez Bravo: 1920–1986,* Paris, Paris Musées/Paris Audio Visuel, 1986.

3. Diese Aufnahme hat einen historischen Vorläufer in O.G. Rejlanders *Der Junggesellentraum* und mindestens einen Nachkommen im drittletzten Bild aus Ralph Gibsons *Déja-Vu.*

NOTES

Cet essai est une version actualisée et élargie de celle parue à l'origine dans *Artforum* en avril 1976, et a été reprise dans *Light Readings* de A.D. Coleman, New York, Oxford University Press.

1. Emily Edwards, *Painted Walls of Mexico : From Prehistoric Times until Today,* photographies de Manuel Alvarez Bravo, Austin, University of Texas Press, 1968, p. 145.

2. Bien qu'épuisé, voir, par exemple, *M. Alvarez Bravo,* de Jane Livingston, Boston et Washington D.C., David R. Godine et the Corcoran Gallery of Art, 1978 ; et *Alvarez Bravo : fotografias 1928-1968,* texte de Juan Gracia Ponce, Mexico, Instituto Nacional des Bellas Artes, D.F. : Comité Organizador de Los Juegos de Las XIX Olympiada, 1968. Des rétrospectives se sont tenues récemment à l'International Center of Photography, New York, et au Musée d'Art Moderne de la Ville de Paris, avec un catalogue de 303 photographies, *Alvarez Bravo : 1920-1986,* Paris, Paris Musées/Paris Audio Visuel, 1986.

3. Cette image précise a son prédécesseur dans « Le rêve du célibataire » d'O. G. Rejlanders, et au moins un rejeton dans la troisième image à partir de la fin de Déjà-Vu de Ralph Gibson.

4. Le lien entretenu par Alvarez Bravo entre lui-même et sa terre imprègne ses images. Il a ainsi écrit : « Je suis né à Mexico, derrière la cathédrale, là où s'élevaient sans doute les temples des anciens

He says of himself, "I was born in the city of Mexico, behind the Cathedral, in the place where the temples of the ancient Mexican gods must have been built, February fourth, 1902." In Fred R. Parker, *Manuel Alvarez Bravo,* Pasadena, California: Pasadena Art Museum, 1971, p. 48.

4. Alvarez Bravos Bindung an dieses Land durchdringt seine Bilder. Er sagt von sich: »Ich bin am 4. Februar 1902 in Mexico City geboren, hinter der Kathedrale, an dem Platz, an dem die Tempel der alten mexikanischen Götter erbaut worden sein müssen.« In: Fred R. Parker, *Manuel Alvarez Bravo,* Pasadena, Kalifornien, Pasadena Art Museum, 1971, S. 48.

dieux mexicains, le 4 février 1902. » Fred R. Parker, *Manuel Alvarez Bravo,* Pasadena, Californie, Pasadena Art Museum, 1971, p. 48.

Retrato desagradable, 1945

La de las Bellas Artes, 1933–34

El trapo negro, 1986

Retrato de lo eterno, 1935

Caballo de madera, 1928

Día de todos los muertos, 1933

Obrero en huelga, asesinado, 1934

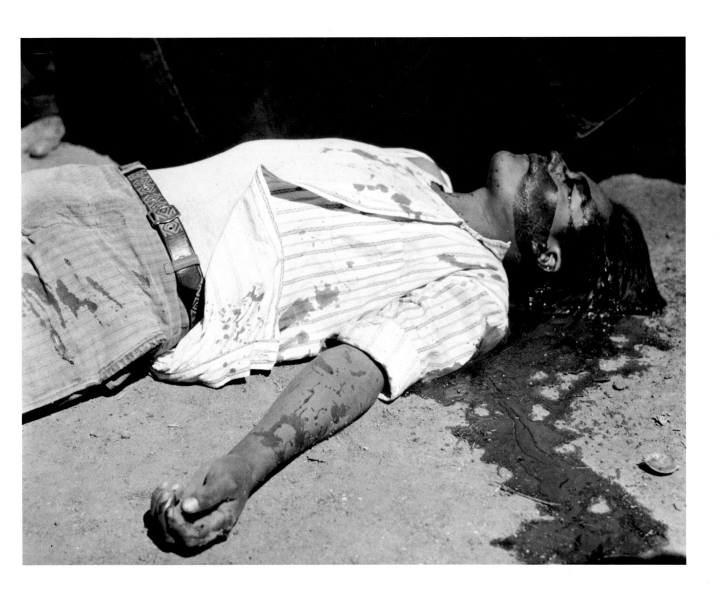

Corona de espinas, 1925

61

Los creadores, los formadores, 1940–42

63

Ángeles en camión, 1930

Niño maya de Tulum, 1942

Retrato póstumo, 1939

Un poco alegre y graciosa, 1942

El ensueño, 1931

El perro veinte, 1958

Luz restirada, 1947

Coronada de palmas, 1936

La quema, 1957

Salinero, 1939

Trabajadores del trópico, 1944

Trampa puesta, c1930

	BRIEF CHRONOLOGY	KURZBIOGRAPHIE	BRÈVE BIOGRAPHIE
1902	Born February 4, Mexico City.	Geboren am 4. Februar in Mexico City.	Naît à Mexico, le 4 févier.
1915 –16	Quits school and works as a copy clerk.	Verlässt die Schule und arbeitet als Büroangestellter.	Quitte l'école et travaille comme employé de bureau.
1916 –30	Works for the Mexican Treasury Department in various capacities.	Arbeitet in diversen Eigenschaften für das Mexican Treasury Department.	Occupe différentes fonctions au Mexican Treasury Department.
1917 –18	Takes night classes in literature; also studies painting and music at the Academia Nacional de Bellas Artes de San Carlos.	Besucht Abendkurse in Literatur; studiert Malerei und Musik an der Academia Nacional de Bellas Artes de San Carlos.	Prend des cours du soir en littérature; étudie également la musique et la peinture à l'Academia Nacional de Bellas Artes de San Carlo.
1922	First becomes interested in photography and the indigenous art of Mexico.	Interessiert sich erstmals für Fotografie und die mexikanische Volkskunst.	S'intéresse à la photographie et à l'art populaire mexicain.
1923	Meets the German photographer Hugo Brehme.	Begegnet dem deutschen Fotografen Hugo Brehme.	Rencontre le photographe allemand Hugo Brehme.
1924	Buys his first camera and takes portraits of his colleagues.	Kauft seine erste Kamera und macht Porträts von seinen Kollegen.	Achète son premier appareil photo, et prend des portraits de ses collègues.
1926	Wins first prize at a regional exposition in Oaxaca.	Gewinnt den ersten Preis bei einer regionalen Ausstellung in Oaxaca.	Remporte le premier prix d'une exposition régionale à Oaxaca.
1927	Meets the photographer Tina Modotti who encourages his work.	Lernt die Fotografin Tina Modotti kennen, die ihn in seiner Arbeit ermutigt.	Rencontre la photographe Tina Modotti qui l'encourage dans ses travaux.
1929	Instructor in Photography, Escuela Central de Artes Plásticas. At instigation of Modotti, sends some work to Edward Weston, who encourages him to continue in photography. Meets Rufino Tamayo.	Lehrer für Fotografie an der Escuela Central de Artes Plásticas. Sendet auf Anregung Modottis einige Arbeiten an Edward Weston, der ihn ermutigt, weiter zu fotografieren. Lernt Rufino Tamayo kennen.	Instructeur en photographie à l'Escuela Central de Artes Plásticas. À l'instigation de Modotti, envoie quelques travaux à Edward Weston qui l'encourage à continuer. Rencontre Rufino Tamayo.
1930	Quits job at the Ministry of Finance; becomes freelance photographer. Through Modotti and Frances Toor, editor of *Mexican Folkways,* meets Mexican muralists, including Diego Rivera, David Alfaro Siqueiros, José Clemente Orozco, and photographs their work for the next several years.	Gibt die Stellung im Finanzministerium auf; wird freischaffender Fotograf. Lernt über Modotti und Frances Toor, den Herausgeber von *Mexican Folkways,* mexikanische Wandmaler kennen, darunter Diego Rivera, David Alfaro Siqueiros und José Clemente Orozco, deren Arbeiten er im Laufe der folgenden Jahre fotografiert.	Quitte son poste au Ministère des Finances. Devient photographe indépendant. À travers Modotti et Frances Toor, éditeur de *Mexican Folkways,* rencontre des fresquistes mexicains, dont Diego Rivera, David Alfaro Siqueiros, José Clemente Orozco. Il photographie leurs œuvres au cours des années qui suivent.
1931	Receives First Prize, *concurso de fotografía,* Fábrica de Cemento, La Tolteca.	Erhält den ersten Preis im *concurso de fotografía* der Fábrica de Cemento in La Tolteca.	Reçoit le Premier prix du *concurso de fotografía* de la Fábrica de Cemento, La Tolteca.
1938 –40	Professor of photography at the Academia Nacional de Bellas Artes de	Professor für Fotografie an der	Professeur de photographie à l'Academia Nacional de Bellas Artes de

San Carlos. Meets André Breton and becomes interested in surrealism.

1940 -42 RUNS a commercial photography studio in Mexico City.

1943 -59 WORKS as photographer and camera operator for Sindicato de Trabajadores de la Producción Cinematográfica de México.

1959 WITH Leopoldo Mendez, Rafael Carrillo, and Carlos Pellicer, founds Fondo Editorial de la Plástica Mexicana, with the goal of publishing books on Mexican art.

1974 RECEIVES the Sourasky Art Prize.

1975 RECEIVES the National Art Prize (Mexico) and a John Simon Guggenheim Memorial Fellowship.

1976 THE MUSEO de Arte Moderno, Mexico City, installs a room devoted to a selection of his work, which is on display through 1982.

1980 LEAVES Fondo Editorial de la Plástica Mexicana to develop a Mexican Museum of Photography. Becomes honorary member of the Academia de Artes, Mexico.

1984 RECEIVES the Swedish Victor and Erna Hasselblad Prize.

1986 THE MUSEUM of Mexican Photography opens March 26. Receives Brehm Memorial Award from the Rochester Institute of Technology.

1987 HONOURED as Master of Photography by the International Center of Photography.

1994 RECEIVES the Peer Award for Distinguished Career in Photography from Friends of Photography, San Francisco

---

Academia Nacional de Bellas Artes de San Carlos. Lernt André Breton kennen und beginnt, sich für den Surrealismus zu interessieren.

BETREIBT ein kommerzielles Fotostudio in Mexico City.

ARBEITET als Fotograf und Kameramann für das Sindicato de Trabajadores de la Producción Cinematográfica de México .

GRÜNDET mit Leopoldo Mendez, Rafael Carrillo und Carlos Pellicer den Fondo Editorial de la Plástica Mexicana mit dem Ziel, Bücher über mexikanische Kunst zu verlegen.

ERHÄLT den Sourasky-Kunstpreis.

ERHÄLT den Nationalen Kunstpreis von Mexiko und ein John Simon Guggenheim Stipendium.

DAS MUSEO de Arte Moderno, Mexico City, richtet einen Raum ein, der einer Auswahl seiner Werke gewidmet ist; sie sind bis 1982 durchgängig zu sehen.

VERLÄSST den Fondo Editorial de la Plástica Mexicana, um ein Mexikanisches Museum für Fotografie aufzubauen. Wird Ehrenmitglied der Academia de Artes, Mexiko.

ERHÄLT den schwedischen Victor-und-Erna-Hasselblad-Preis.

AM 26. März eröffnet das Museum für Mexikanische Fotografie. Erhält den Brehm Memorial Award vom Rochester Institute of Technology.

WIRD vom International Center of Photography als Master of Photography geehrt.

ERHÄLT den Peer Award for Distinguished Career in Photography von den Friends of Photography, San Francisco

---

San Carlos. Rencontre André Breton et s'intéresse au surréalisme.

TIENT un studio de photographie commerciale à Mexico.

TRAVAILLE comme photographe et cameraman pour le Sindicato de Trabajadores de la Producción Cinematográfica de México.

AVEC Leopoldo Mendez, Rafael Carrillo et Carlos Pellicer, crée le Fondo Editorial de la Plástica Mexicana, pour éditer des livres sur l'art mexicain.

REÇOIT le Prix Sourasky.

REÇOIT le Prix National des Arts (Mexique) et une bourse John Simon Guggenheim.

LE MUSEO de Arte Moderno de Mexico, ouvre une salle consacrée à son œuvre jusqu'en 1982.

QUITTE le Fondo Editorial de la Plástica Mexicana pour créer un Musée mexicain de la photographie. Devient membre honoraire de l'Academia de Artes, Mexico.

REÇOIT le Prix suédois Victor et Erna Hasselblad.

LE MUSÉE de la photographie mexicaine ouvre le 26 mars. Reçoit le Brehm Memorial Award du Rochester Institute of Technology.

L'INTERNATIONAL Center of Photography lui rend hommage.

REÇOIT le Peer Award for Distinguished Career in Photography des Friends of Photography, San Francisco

SELECTED EXHIBITIONS
AUSGEWÄHLTE
AUSSTELLUNGEN
EXPOSITIONS SÉLECTIONNÉES

1926 Oaxaca, Mexico, regional
exhibition.

1932 Galería Posada, Mexico City.

1935 Palacio de Bellas Artes, Mexico
City. With Henri Cartier-Bresson.
Julien Levy Gallery, New York. With
Walker Evans and Henri Cartier-
Bresson.

1936 Hull House, Chicago.

1939 Galerie Renou et Colle, Paris,
Souvenir du Mexique. Retrospective
exhibition of Mexican art organized
by André Breton.
Universidad Nacional de Mexico,
Mexico City.

1940 Galería de Arte Mexicano (Galería
Inés Amor), Mexico City, *Exposición
Internacional del Surrealismo.*

1942 Photo League, New York.

1943 Philadelphia Museum of Art,
Mexican Art Today. Art Institute of
Chicago.

1945 Sociedad de Arte Moderno, Mexico
City, *Manuel Alvarez Bravo – Fotografías.*
Catalog with essays by Manuel Alvarez
Bravo, Diego Rivera, Xavier
Villaurrutia, and Gabriel Figueroa.
Museum of Modern Art, New York,
with Paul Strand, Walker Evans, and
August Sander.

1955 Museum of Modern Art, New
York, *The Family of Man,* world tour
through 1959.

1957 Salón de la Plástica Mexicana.

1966 Galería de Arte Mexicano (Galería
Inés Amor), Mexico City.

1968 Palacio Nacional de Bellas Artes,
Mexico City, XIX Olympiad. *Manuel
Alvarez Bravo – Fotografías 1928 – 1968.*

1971 Pasadena Art Museum. Museum of
Modern Art, New York.

1972 Witkin Gallery, New York. Palacio
Nacional de Bellas Artes, Mexico
City, *Manuel Alvarez Bravo: 400
fotografías.*

1973 Casa de la Cultura, Juchitán.

1974 Galería José Clemente Orozco,
Mexico, *Cien fotografías y paisajes
inventados.* Art Institute of Chicago.
From the collection of the Instituto
Nacional de Bellas Artes, Mexico City
and the Palacio Nacional de Bellas
Artes. Travels to the University of
Massachusetts Art Gallery.

1975 Museo de Arte Moderno, Caracas.
Witkin Gallery, New York. Galería
Juan Martín, Mexico. Pan Opticon
Gallery, Boston.

1976 La Photogalerie, Paris. Travels to
Musée Nicéphore Niepce, Chalon-
sur-Saône and the Galerie Municipale
du Château d'Eau, Toulouse. Museo
de Arte Moderno, Mexico City.

1977 Galería Juan Martín, Mexico City.
Photographer's Gallery, London.
Corcoran Gallery, Washington.
Travels. University of Arizona,
Tucson, *Contemporary Photography in
Mexico.*

1979 Musée Réattu, Arles, *Rencontres
Internationales de la Photographie.*

1980 Galerie Agathe Gaillard, Paris.
Academia de Artes de Mexico.

1981 Witkin Gallery, New York.

1982. Museo de Arte Moderno, Mexico
City.

1983 Israel Museum, Jerusalem. Travels
to the New Museum, Bradford, the
Museum of Modern Art, Oxford, and
Photographer's Gallery, London.

1984 Third Colloqium of Latin
American Photography, Havana.

1985 Salas Pablo Ruiz Picasso, Biblioteca
Nacional, Madrid.

1986 Galería de Exposiciones del Palacio
de Bellas Artes, Mexico City. *Fiftieth
anniversary exhibition* with Henri
Cartier-Bresson.
Hartnett Gallery, Rochester Institute
of Technology. Musée d'Art Moderne
de la Ville de Paris.

1987 International Center of
Photography, New York.

1988 Alla and Sheinbaum and Russek
Gallery, Santa Fe, New Mexico.

1989 The Within Gallery, New York.
Centro Cultural Arte.
Contemporaneo, Mexico. *Mudo Sol,*
Bellas Artes, Mexico. Museo de Arte
Moderno, Buenos Aires.

1990 Museum of Photographic Arts, San
Diego, California.

1992 *90th Birthday Exhibition,* Galería
Juan Martín, Mexico. The Within
Gallery, New York. Musée de l'Elysée,
Lausanne.

1996 Museo de Arte Moderno, Mexico.
Museo Nacional Centro de Arte
Reina Sofía, Madrid.

SELECTED BIBLIOGRAPHY
AUSGEWÄHLTE BIBLIOGRAPHIE
SÉLECTION BIBLIOGRAPHIQUE

1930 Maximo Brétal. Untitled article. *Excelsior* (Mexico) November 13.

1935 *Manuel Alvarez Bravo.* Text by Luis Cardoza y Aragón and Langston Hughes. Mexico City.

1937 Bertram D. Wolfe and Diego Rivera. *Portrait of Mexico.* New York: Covici Friede. Photographs by Alvarez Bravo, Tina Modotti, and Lupercio.

1939 André Breton. "Souvenir du Mexique." *Minotaure* (Paris) 3 (12–13): 29–52 (May).
Benjamin Péret. "Ruines: Ruine des Ruines." *Minotaure* (Paris) 3 (12–13): 57 (May).
Xavier Villaurrutia. "Manuel Alvarez Bravo." *Artes Plásticas* (Mexico) 1 (Spring).

1945 David Alfaro Siqueiros. "Movimiento y Meneos de Arte en México." *ASI* (Mexico) 249 (August 18): 12–13.

1953 Minor White. "Manuel Alvarez Bravo." *Aperture* 1 (4): 28–36.

1966 Emily Edwards. *Painted Walls of Mexico.* Austin: University of Texas Press. Photographs by Manuel Alvarez Bravo.
Margarita Nelken. "Manuel Alvarez Bravo." *Excelsior* (Mexico) June 3.
William Philip Spratling. *More Human Than Divine.* Mexico City: Universidad Nacional Autonome de Mexico.

1968 *Manuel Alvarez Bravo Fotografías 1928–1968.* Mexico City: Instituto Nacional de Bellas Artes. Selection of poems text by Juan García Ponce.
Paul Strand. "Manuel Alvarez Bravo." *Aperture* 13 (4): 2–12.

1970 Robin Grace. "Manuel Alvarez Bravo." *Album* (London) 9: 2–14 (October).

1971 David Cordoni. "Manuel Alvarez Bravo." *Artweek* 4 (24): 9–10 (July 7).
John Littlewood. "Bravo's Mexican Pictures: Photographic Timelessness." *Christian Science Monitor* April 5, p. 22.
Fred R. Parker. *Manuel Alvarez Bravo.* Pasadena: Pasadena Art Museum.
Leland Rice. "Mexico's Master Photographer." *Artweek* 4 (20): 22 (May 22).

1972 Fred R. Parker. "Manuel Alvarez Bravo." *Camera* (Lucerne) 51: 34–43 (January).

1974 Richard Pare. "Manuel Alvarez Bravo – Hieratic Images of Life and Death." *New Art Examiner* (Chicago) 1 (7): 9 (April).

1975 Michael André. "Photography: Manuel Alvarez Bravo." *ArtNews* 74 (7): 104 (September).
"El Arte Fotografico de Manuel Alvarez Bravo." *Revista de Bellas Artes* (Mexico) January – February.
Salvador Elizondo. "Manuel Alvarez Bravo." *Plural* (Mexico) 4 (11): 5, 77–78 (August).
Gene Thornton. "The Mexico of Alvarez Bravo." *New York Times* May 25, sec. 2, p. 25.
Peter Turner. "Manuel Alvarez Bravo" *Creative Camera International Yearbook,* eds. Colin Osman and Peter Turner. London: Coo Press, pp. 10–36.
Anne Middleton Wagner. "Manuel Alvarez Bravo at the University of Massachusetts Art Gallery." *Art in America* 63 (3): 77–78 (May–June).

1976 Gerry Badger. "The Labyrinth of Solitude: The Art of Manuel Alvarez Bravo." *The British Journal of Photography* 123 (6043): 425–428 (May 21).

A.D. Coleman. "The Indigenous Vision of Manuel Alvarez Bravo." *Artforum* 14 (8): 60–63 (April).
Michel Nuridsany. "Le Mexique sans folklore d' Alvarez Bravo." *Le Figaro,* April 26.
Octavio Paz. "Cara al Tiempo." *Plural* (Mexico) 58 (July): 43–45.
Martine Voyeux. "Voir, c'est un vice." *Le Quotidien de Paris,* May 13.

1977 Paul Hill and Tom Cooper. "Manuel Alvarez Bravo." *Camera* 56 (5): 36–38 (May); 56 (8): 35–36 (August).

1978 Jessica Alonso. "From the Soul of Mexico to the Heart of America." *Boston Globe,* March 29.
Stu Cohen. "Photography: Shooting the Heart of Mexico." *Boston Phoenix,* April 4, sec. 3, p. 9.
Jane Livingston et al. *M. Alvarez Bravo.* Boston: Godine, and Washington, DC: Corcoran Gallery of Art.
Joan Murray. "Manuel Alvarez Bravo: 'Como Siempre.'" *Artweek* 9 (19): 1, 11 (May 13).
René Verdugo and Terrence Pitts. "Manuel Alvarez Bravo." *Contemporary Photography in Mexico.* Tucson: University of Arizona.

1980 Vivienne Silver. *The Artistic Development and Evolution of Manuel Alvarez Bravo, Mexican Photographer, As Seen Through His Nudes.* Master thesis, University of Arizona.

1983 Octavio Paz. *Instante y Revelación.* Mexico: Fonapas-Círculo Editorial. Texts and poems with photographs by Manuel Alvarez Bravo.
Nissan N. Perez and Ian Jeffrey. *Dreams, Visions, Metaphors.* Jerusalem: Israel Museum.

1987 *Manuel Alvarez Bravo.* Paris: Paris Musées/Paris Audio Visuel.

Cuarto para las doce, 1957

APERTURE MASTERS OF PHOTOGRAPHY